Decades of Experience

Decades of Experience

Love, Life & Laughter

Cristina "BL!ss" Calderon

To order additional copies of this book, contact:
Xlibris Corporation
1-888-795-4274
www.Xlibris.com
Orders@Xlibris.com
92516

Contents

A Poem 4 Whom

[Written May 6th, 2008 @ 1:15pm]

Recommended doses seem
To analyze too much
Every little touch can
Be liked or as such
Yearning to balance our
Needs takes time
Hand over the keys
If you even had wine
Neglect nothing when we nod
Our heads
Every little sentence
Seems to repeat what I've said

Each little creature
Sees endless bumps in the road
We chide them
For being lumps
When all along
It was our big dumps
Invading the clues
Like a pack of chumps . . .

Loving each moment
Young and free
Only thing holding me back
Underground monotony

Billionaire Mansion, Bigger

[Written 24 Aug 2009 @ 12:24 P.M.]

In 2003-2004, this one opened up
An amazing door! But the
Windows were shut and the
Back way, too; so, few breezes
Were able to make it through.

The house that we built,
Brick by brick; on friendship
Love & honor ship, was missin'
The vents and the glue to
Stick. Stale air stifles
Caring, sharing heart
To tick.

We picked out
Paints, nicknamed our
Neighbors. And, before dark
Talked out our angers-and
All frustration's set aside.
Closed our eyes, Thanked God
For the countryside. We ride
Through town on one high horse;
Well, pushin' 600 'cause it's a Porsche
On top of the world like Brandy
Sings—Earnin' our keep, yep!
Earnin' our wings.

Since you asked, exactly, the
Dimensions, of my love
And satisfaction, I would
Say, my first reaction, is
Billionaire's mansion bigger,
Fed'ral Reserve backin'!

All my transactions, transgressions are
Known. I'd like to hit ya up
On my cellular phone. You said
'We have chemistry' when we
Were alone. And, yes, we can
Name our first daughter, Joan!

I've prepared, in bliss, our paths meet more;
To our prayers being answered, joy days in store!

City of Alpha Bets

[Written 7-10 Nov 2008]

A, you took care as I departed, fair
Your flair, I was aware
Kept me right there.
B, I love you, though our times were few
Why did you undo the-bridge-I-made to you?

C, so clearly and dearly we met,
Heaven-sent, though hell-bent on staying content.
D, two times, you slapped my face
And did not replace
My happy face or fun race.

E, you showed me excess ain't best,
But, I passed your test and stayed out west.
F was a friend and now you love bends
In our roads may depend on who you amend.

G! My true image of what I do see
In the butt of history's jokes
On rut's mystery.
H, in my hat, had me take a step back, You cut me some slack In the area
I once lacked

I do care about you,
Helpin' makin' skies blue
And that familiar hue
Of red, my bra ya undo,
Undid, K, I did, love you and your kids.
If I put in a bid for your heart, would you give?
L, a call is all that I asked
You surpassed the task and now, I'm free at last!
M and M and N, O, P, went so freely,
I skipped a beat and slowly
Proceeded to thank thee.
Q, you do always amaze me.

How come booze was #3 to your kids and work, G?
Ya see, R, I respect thee way you attack,
Never from the back and your
Perfect rack on pool tables,
You smack! And, kind S, for the snack time treat,
Your timing was neat
And you didn't retreat when my heart skipped the heat of

T's desire, you are a live squire,
Though, on the line, you fire
And hit the right wire.

U knew from day one, how to find
Our good fun, at the range, with your gun,
I killed your record of one,
Shot!
One thrill, V, my motives, you fill
Into oblivion spill.
Thanks for all the good will.

W is the side of me, I distance
Myself from a part of G-status
Is the maddest
Pre-adolescence misery.

X was how you signed your name
For a good time, you lacked the blame
I tried so hard, you remained same.
Now, who's the one who's really sane?

Y, oh why do you still call?
You push, I fall;
I jump, you stall.
. . . You are not down for it all.

Z, you forget, without A, there's no bet,
I've done my time,
No regret and without a safety net.

Thank you for your time
No, thank you, for the wine
Without it, I was fine
Don't again involve the swine
Piggly wiggly time is for kids
Just quit blowin' off the lids
Of the slimier than squids
Don't attack her, for she rids . . .
ME! Of my agony, SHe prevents
Insanity
AND, is ingrained in history
And keeps me from
Beating hypocrites I see.

Extra Ordinary Boy

[Written 09 Aug 2009]

Men, around me, who to look up to?
Ironic, it seems, the Vets in
Cold sewers blew—changing from,
How's-it-feel-to-be norm?
Announce soldier form;
Erase, Bleed, move on.
Lack the need to take it personal

Jump the ship or eat bland cereal
Aware their 'Hip days' means MRI
Cryin', sittin' in a ditch, questionin' why
Kept up souls don't bleed remorse
Slave souls, though, beat that dead horse
Onward, soldier, here's your sign
Neglect scars can heal, you're doin' fine!

Extra Ordinary boy, keep your open mind
Your Love is secure and you soon will find
Pretty paces in a row, set your course at ease
You can swim wit the fishes
Or fly like birds through trees.

Temptation is set up, like a trap
Widen angles of your perspective snap-
Shots are carefully called
Plans transform to results,
You can gripe all alone or
Call those friend catapults,
There's keys-to-life-best
Learned on-a-team.
Caring individuals
Know 'bout love supreme.
Laying down your life for a
Brother is just as sweet
As Love from a Mother.

I've got your back
Thanks, for havin' mine
Family, forever
Drinkin' victory wine.
    I'm fine all of the time
    You do inspire my rhyme.
    Boom, Bah Da boom!

Garden of Life

[Written 8 Jul 2008]

Intelligence is guessed

Time constraints are myths and tests

Seems we all have our cues
Now, some won't pay their dues

On a whim, I've seen some change
Tyrants try to not behave
Whether good or bad, a life some never have

Happiness is fluid, and I know I've seen you do it

Aware of cause, effect, that smile I do detect

Timid smirk tells me so much,
Yet, little I can't touch

Or the opposite is true
Under umbrella of blue

Restraints can't hold me down
Even keel with my frown

And hang me upside down, you'll see
Ponder all my history, you still won't
Believe, thee generosity

Unfolds with the rain, some say I
Take trains to keep me sane and
Happy, but I'm comforted by
One place, my home, the garden
Will bring forth patience

You may not understand it
Or think I love my planet

Unconditionally too much

Seriously, at will
Omni-directional, I arise to a challenge

Worlds wont' come between me
And my passion for where I
Now stand, my family's the right
Digits of my hand, times this
When you threaten my clan
Havoc comes in a fist, not mine, though I
Advance after foot soldiers clear
The only chance you once had
You are NOT my dad, and you will see
Overhead, the birds are all glad

Under them, you'll feel moist
Great to see your fine choice
Run away, 'cause nature's got mine

Omnipotent back won't break just yet
When kids keep me on my toes and jet.

Green And Brown

[Written 19 May 2008]

When your face hits the ground,
From a trip or a fall

I know what cushions
And I've felt the stall
Of dirt in my nostrils,
Dirt in my nails

I hope pails of water will wash it away.

I ate the green grass and vegs
'Cause it healed my stomach
The grass, serene
I spit out dirt & liked it

'Cause I know that it don't hurt,
Unless you only inhale it
Then, the nostrils, cut off from air,
Lose care.

Sometimes, a box stops
The ground 'cause it consumes
All those around
Who do not move
But, sit and wait
I'm glad there's no time
For me to sit, as bait.

I hid in green but moved serene
I churned the dirt
Making it work
For, not against
And, my enemies fled
Now, I'm safe and sound in bed.

I Believe

[Written Saturday, December 08, 2007]

I'm drowning, here!
But no one will throw me a rope . . .

Each time I try to be a good friend
Like all before, they burn me in the end.
I try to hide from the isht, but I'm right under the fan
Exactly what gives? I do not understand.

Victory to who when you are both on your knees
Ending the charade to hide how it bleeds.

Internal Vision

[Written 12 Oct 2000 at 8:30 P.M.]

The worlds beyond us are not known
And worlds below us made of foam
Keep us pondering, both ourselves
Encased in that also suppose
Nymphs and faeries of fantasies

Frolic freely far in the trees.
Of here and oft where humans not
Restricted by blank document

Granting nothing to us mortals
Reaching some of endless portals
Always hoping evidence lies
Nowhere but in our alibis
Truth never fully revealed
Exceptions found both in the field
Deep sea has too the answers we

Each day pursue to find the key
Very close we will seem to come
Enthralled to me, then come undone
Really, I think we should not stare
You can't change it, it hurts to care

Triumphant only in our hearts
Inside we gave up many parts
Make matters worse I do not know
Each second counts
      When there's the glow

2007/12/02 15:08

Minor Details AKA
THC Deficiency/ Cancer prevention

[Written 26 Nov 2000, Sunday 8:30 P.M.]

So, there's something missing in my life?
Well, I'm alive without it, so how could I be missing it . . .
Oh, the pain its absence leaves.
That could be it.

But, I can handle the pain,
I SAID I CAN TAKE IT, WHY,
YOU don't THINK I CAN?!?

It MIGHT seem I'm near losing my head, here, but
Honestly, I'm fine.
Really, there is no need to be worried.

I'm just not receiving enough oxygen to my heart.
Does my heart even need that extra stuff?
I thought it thrived on BLOOD,
Is my blood not good enough?
Oh, snap! It's the anemic qualities, isn't it,
Or no, my biological make up is not sequenced correctly,
That's why my heart is in so much aching pain, right?

Please tell me some drug is going to take it all away.
My prescription better not say IT'S what's MISSING in
My life . . . what my heart needs!

L   O   V   E ,   J   O   Y—

P   E   A   C   E.

No String Attach

[Written 10 Aug 2009]

Versatile dance partners are so hard to find
Don't worry, they aren't staring
They're just waitin' in line
I'm known to be a catch, of sorts,
Here's signed 8x10 . . .

Born & raised, east of Hollywood
So, movies, I've been in . . .

Last job's music video and TV,
I knew, you-would like the attention,
So, here's my card, too.

I'm just here to dance wit you.
Think of this as a sneak preview,
If available for a rendezvous,
Call those digits
Let's make grey skies blue.

Usher in MJ-RIP-back beat
For years, we chased each other
And you still are sweet,
As the dove from above
Wit olive branch
I'm golden like the girls
Who hung with Blanche!

Catch ya at next dance
    Club, bar, event . . .
Plannin' seein' YOU, again-
Since-you-must-be heaven-sent!

Thanks for the gift
Of your presence,
We are girls on film
Who love the camera.
The few. The proud, who go
The distance.
Make-the-dance pure art,
Head to Canberra;
Or anywhere our hearts can be;
Free as the butterflies up in the tree!

Please Contradict What I See, Hear and Feel

[Written November 2, 2007]

I'm a sleuth at the game, Girls come at me insane
With lies boys speak the same, as they do the dang thang
What it is, I don't know, If you make my sis a ho
Your breath will be no more; it won't be me shutting your door.
Rapists, molesters know your path
I've been brought down by them and laugh
All they do is build my wrath
So you better take a bath
I can smell isht from afar, and I don't even need a car
My speeding bullet is my fist, and I know you won't resist
A chance to prove all that you're worth
But, boy, you are taking on a girl
So your worth has less appeal
To the mainstream, that's why there is jail for obscene
Images you portray, and hey, you won't be made gay
As you stay in the pen and Big Ben makes you his bitch
So, you better switch your walk, and I don't wanna hear you talk
Or move in my den's direction
I practice deflection, as I send you to anotha dimension
My young don't need to see, what a pity one can be

I try to show positively, all that they can be
Take your drugs somewhere else
Cause I value my family's health
And you don't threaten my wealth
Trampin' by thinkin' you're stealth
The grass may somewhat hide
How it is you are so snide
Exit my presence, is all I ask
Repeating myself is like nails on glass
Exhausting my speech to protect my den
Makes me tired and cranky, with men
Who won't let me defend my turf
I was here, first, and am by birth
A shield to keep ill thoughts at bay
I've seen the light and your dismay
You try to lure my loved ones so
They stray from right and then follow
Destructive paths of chaos, death
You break them 'til there's nothing left
That will not happen on my watch
Your evil plan I'll try to botch.

Stream Dream

[Written 20 Jun 2008]

Jumpin' up and down, when that magic hit
   Epiphany came and went, I'm feelin' it
   Now is the time to shine bright as bulbs
Neglecting the "more power" motto from lost sons

Into the thick of all who conquer words
   Forgetting rhymes and doing time in name of turds
   Exactly what builds and breaks the mold
Reality hurts when the lies are told

Careful ones bring the key to free
   Ornery lil' ones stay locked, indeed
   Reach for the heights like P. Service said
Deciding what is good for me, instead

According to the fishes, I'm good to go
   You should taste the precious morsels to know
   What I love is salmon and it helps me grow
Ending my hunger and the bones will sew.

The World

[Written on 15 Jun 2007, just after Midnight]

Nice dreams invade my slumber
And sustain such-
Intelligent thoughts of whom
I love so much-
Keeper or not to
Keep my promises so—

Outstanding ovation
To those that I know

Beautiful words spoken, sang
And wrote down like,
Lovely interludes not
Needing a black mike.
Amazing how simplicity overwhelms me,
Caring individuals
Are all 'round me-
Kind of like heaven
Fulfilled-with-a true glee-
Almost too good
For one to honestly see-

True friends come as
Blue moons
On horizons rare-
Tired of hiding
Their illustrious stare—

Awaken, it's night,
The light
Will fear me not-
Can you believe . . .
    I like to sleep on a cot?
Killing ill wills
In my mind in due time will-
Sustain my existence better than a pill.

Tribe Callings

[Written Monday, January 07, 2008 12:24:51 PM]

Jokin' 'bout the girls I bed, the truth is we just slept instead
I may have gotten in their head, and they may be in mine, I dread.

Like a constant companion without the stress
I'm like a test, only few can pass, the best
Seem lost when in my presence
I know the cost immense

Comin' out the speakers
Hopin' you can hear it

This message of pure bliss
Sounding large, intense

Boomin' loud throughout the tents
If you ignore, then worsened the bets
Are off in the distance
I put up resistance
Knowin' dang well my entrance
Was heard and acknowledged
And utilized my knowledge

Reality is reality and fantasy is our escape
Let's hope our escape is better

Determined to see the light
at the end of this
tunnel vision has got me wishin'
that I was off somewhere fishin'

Up, Under and Around

[Written Cinco de Mayo, of 2010]

Floatin' through the town with ease
Respect the road in front of thee
Each intersection, others use
Exact your path, smooth interlude!

Weary drivers wipe their eyes
Angrys cuss, vain add disguise—
Youth lack miles, Old test the way,
Forgotton roads of yesterday.

Remember check the route ahead,
Engage AFTER a plan is lead.
Execute the gift of reach
Call, if you don't know. Don't screech,
Or go the wrong direction
Many have failed; bad news will mention . . .

Mothers ride, too, also sons
Under the umbrella of family ones
Times two, or three or four
Even those knockin' on heaven's door.

Up, under and around,
Up, Under and Around
Up, under! Up, under!
Up, under and around.

There go scooters, there go bikes. I see grandmas, I hear tykes.

Big rigs rockin' the scene, Harleys! Rumble, so mean!

Choppers barely scrape on by, rice burners, too, flash 'n fly

Soccer mom vans, celeb and rock star fans
Dogs ridin' shottie; top gun engine hottie!

Trains, Barges, seagulls, sparrows . . . here, we all go!

Hallelujah, Praise the Lord
Hallelujah, Praise the Lord
Hallelu! Hallelu! Hallelujah, Praise the Lord!

AAA

[Written 4 Jul 2008]

Since 2001, my heart's been stolen by one
Cruel letter of our alphabet.
Some call number 1.
The order ain't important, but I get it, so much!
It's on my bra; it's on report cards,
Since I learned, breathed and such

An ace in the hole beats queens any day
Even kings hide behind
What brings some dismay.

The jack of all trades is closest to me,
But my enemies are closer,
Kept an eye on, to see
That they don't steal my place, my fate
My demise
I'm first on the list
So, I wear a disguise.

She stole 'U' from us and I'm supposed
To just bust,
Out the door without score,
Only slight lack of trust?

B's got me down, but they holdin'
Me up,
They're corrupt; they erupt like volcanoes blow up.

Should I come to you with a bigger bouquet,
Just to say, you're in top three of my life loves, today?
Or, is a holding pattern your repertoire
Or like a bone, will you keep me locked in your drawer?

Yes, I'm your toy, do with me what you wish
Just know that I grow what is on your dish

So keep going fishing
I hear that you're wishin'
There were more like me
But, there's only room for one
In our history,
Dishing out the kindness like a factory,
Only 10% I've let be seen to thee.

Black & Brown, White & Brown, Red & Blue, Black & Blue, Black & White

[Written 10 Jun 2008]

The scars of youth
Left us thinkin' we were
Bulletproof
We forgot that women helped healing,
I've seen proof.

When you watch her chest
Rise and fall on beat
It reminds me of ebb & flow
And, we're so neat
Completely whole,
When we know our role
Or try to have focus,
When we take a stroll
'Cause those trolls under bridges may collect a fee
Or a fine, you'll have to settle or you won't be free

Women are like a drug
Like when disarmed by a hug
Some love 'em, some hate 'em
But, all came from them & above

All else, we're humans, not gender
The sender of ill repute may not be a bender
If one don't flex, many may break
So TAKE a second to KNOW who holds you & who you take
To the TOP
Or bottom of your solo glass
I'll pass you on up,
If I can't see through
    your past.

Crashing Down

[Written Saturday, August 11, 2007, at 10:44 AM]

When one loses a parent, it can be a difficult situation. Death is a powerful force which may take a parent out of one's life. Circumstance also may affect one's parent's accessibility. Distance is another obstacle that gets between parent/child relationships. Overcoming these situations may take substantial time to accomplish. Sometimes, we never seem to get over it.

What happens when you lose your parent(s) at a young age? Without embracing the change, many children become lost, forever looking for that parent or parents. Some find other things to preoccupy the time not spent with their parents, like booze or drugs. The pain and grief felt is immense. Alcohol, drugs and anything to excess may help to temporarily ease the pain. It feels like there is a giant hole in one's heart, where the love of that parent is supposed to fit, and if they are not there to give that love, the darkness of the hole feels like it spreads over the entire heart.

Perhaps, when one finds a life partner, that hole is filled. A different kind of love takes the place of the missing parent's love. It may feel like a temporary patch, or a puzzle piece that nearly fits perfectly. And then, when that life partner is no more, you can sometimes replace them with a new one. Other times, it feels like that was the only puzzle piece to fit in that gaping hole in one's heart. Now, one is left with a hole as big as the ocean is wide.

Lost love is hard to forget. Forgiveness should be in order, but to forget the love feels impossible. How does one go on when the love is not there? What happens when you lose the love and many factors led to the loss? Can we fight these factors, so that they do not take our love and throw it out like old garbage? One must learn from history and experience, so that history does not repeat itself. The love can be found, again, in different experiences. That same love may be revisited, in dreams or reality, but it never seems to feel the way it did in the beginning.

Fast from Mass Media

[Written December 5, 2007]
1-1-1-1

From Saturday, December 1st to Sunday, December 2nd, I refrained from any mass media influences. Since I do not, typically, receive much mass media, it was an easy task. To start things off, my little sister and I attended a Christmas parade in Whittier. Then, I went for a walk. Afterwards, we drove around in my Aunt's car, while I listened to a CD that I need to listen to for my music class, American Popular Music.

Saturday night, I did not do anything, since I have no car, at the moment. On Sunday, I walked to the post office to send a letter to my pen pal. I walked to my sister's work, from there, and borrowed her car to drive to church, where we read from the Bible.

After church, my best friend picked me up and we went on a hike, with his dog, in Santiago Canyon. We traversed the hilly terrain until we arrived at the dam. We hiked up the path to the mountainous trail, nearby. The trail led us to the Barham ridge, where we took many photographs, for my geography class. Many paw prints were left in the mud, as we passed the fire damaged parts of this area.

At the end of this fast, I felt refreshed and warm. Things were going by slower. I stopped to appreciate things more. I did not rush out, after the fast, to break it. In fact, I don't think I've watched television but once since the fast. I did sleep well. I finished up my homework for my other classes, and I even studied for my new job training course. All in all, it was time well spent and I plan on doing more fasts of this nature, often. This assignment showed how many people rely on the media to inform them. I look to the sky and my surrounding environment to tell me what is going on around me. It feels right.

Glow Deep

[Written 12 Jun 2010]

Launched the yacht
Above-Beyond Fever caught
Unleashing true gifts to
Goodness seekers' LOT—
Happy within, the timing,
Saved by Him! My will and
My whims are guided, I win.
In Christ, I thrive and
Love provides. By road & or sky
Energy does survive! I go the
Knots, I push the distance,
Nimble cracked pots shine
On this instance of
Worlds-quite-unseen to un-
Trained eye.
I believe
And-have-since-
At LEAST
Ninety-Five.
26 years still
Isn't enough
Barely scratchin'
The surface of
The Good
Book of Love

Grounded High

[Written 25 Mar 2009]

If you're my soul mate, All I got is love!
I bite my tongue more than most suppose;
And, peace to you and yours, a hug!
Raes of the Son warm me, eyes close.

Following disaster blindly?
I say, No, but, thank you, kindly
Nigeria is where you'll find me and
Determined warriors who bind thee
Gates of heaven to any lost souls
Love life and the Master controls.

Onward, Soldier,
The troops are ready
Realize victory is rockin' steady
Youth, many have got a piece
Tantalizing, though incomplete
Reach new heights, like song before
Understand simply, you must open the door

[written 9 Sept 2009]
Time heals as it reads off of pages
Hear news-boy-yell-it-out for slave's wages
Shift of wealth, kingdoms renewed
Got my health, like the grass, dewed!
Birds still singin', got their fill
Deer are sprinting up the hill

Cloud 9 is a tenth
Of the way I feel
Happiness restored,
Your love's so surreal
Timing is a varied key.
Perfect, in you, is all I see.

I Don't Think That It's True

[Written on 18 Jul 2008]

Love can be found in the bay
I don't think that it's true
Love survives, come what may
I don't see that it's true

Love will find a way, they say
In that old school tune
It's for the birds, I say
As I turn up my Zune
Or iPod, or A-Rod, whatever
Will drown the sound out that
Pounds on the nerves, if I
Was drivin', I'd swerve.

Just keep it simple, my mind don't know
Any other speed but go, unless true
Love will I flow . . . water is love
Love is fluid, fluid flows with
Its surroundings. Astounding
Things come to place when we
Don't race, only pause to
Get a taste, never stare
A questioned face.

I thought I told you
I don't think that it's true
When you said, "I love you"
My poor ears were just blue
I heard olive juice
And left for the store
You thought I answered, not
When I came back
You locked the door and you pushed
Me out of your heart where mine's
Trapped inside. No, I don't
Want it back, I glide
Between there, and here
But my vision's blurry
When you drink beer, and
You forget, you were the one to steer.

Is Served Raw?

[Written 20 Jun 2008]

Tide covers my tracks,
The attacker does not see.
All my skills, he lacks
I sting as the bumble bee.

Swiftly, through the brush, I hide.
He sees what I leave for him.
This is quite a wild ride,
And to think, it's on a whim.

Slow and steady sounds the sea
Behind
My distant memory
And the enemy draws near my kind
To test what we can be.

Closing on him, my young salivate.
Wolf pack won't lack dinner, tonight,
This poor creature's history,
And my youngest sees her chance
To strike
   And protect me,
Project our hunger on this day,
To another way.
All jump in
Right after, though,
It looks a disaster, we now will survive

Music Heals

[Written 15 Jan 1998]

It slowly drips
  Into my soul

Makes me feel good
  Fills my whole

Entity of what
  Is me.

Sears through my
  Blood so smoothly

It lifts me up
  Makes me feel awe

Desire so strong
  Too much I saw.

Without my "drug"
  Nothing am I

I yearn for it
  I even cry.

If I don't hear
  My melody
I just break down
  Fall helplessly

To what I call
  My "great demise"

Silence should fall
  Won't be too wise.

I'll go insane,
  Lose my hair.

Whatever it takes,
  I don't care.

I need it in
  My daily life
Or else my days
  Will fill with strife.

Ecstasy is all I feel
  Forget all things, fake & real.

Forever played would
  Be true bliss
Even better than
  The sweetest kiss.

I'll not forget
  The first time.

My ears were
  Blessed, with rhyme.

Music is the
  Life of me.
Keeps me ticking,
  Sets me free!

Ought To Be

[Written 10 Sept 2008]

Stills my cluttered mind
Eases all the pain, I find
New beginnings, reap rewards
Severs weighted cords and hoards

Umbrella of relief
Ongoing defeat and deflect
Undetecting souls, find them weary
So close to losing

Control or knowing their role by
Announcing what makes one whole
No one thing brings balance back
No one knows the list of lack, except
A chosen entity or a given philosophy
Be it you or be it me,
I know my life's sustained in Thee
Saviour of my wretched soul. The one whom I

Choose and let patrol . . . systems
Seem all at a go when I
Trust in the Lord and just let go
Of what holds back the "good" floodgates.

When I toil in my soil, burying hates
Then feeding unconditional love to mates

Of blood,
Some-sweat, most-tears-
From-years
Of-broken-dates

Honor in loving all feels good.
My life is on the line, it's understood.
My courage grew up, when bold, I stood
For my country, for my brethren
And sisterhood.

Road Map, Guide to Driving: Expanded

[Written 01 Aug 2008]

What moves you?
How do you best get around?
The only reason I ask
Is that I've seen you in town,
And since we on the same route,
I'd like to know what's yours about.

I like to go fast,
But I don't have the cash to fly past
The station with the gas potion,
So I putt around
From spot to spot,
Hoping I don't get caught with wheels,
But no fuel, or in arguments or a duel.

But, I drool over big trucks.
They can make me go nuts
When traversing hard roads,
When avoiding green toads,
When deciphering codes.

I chose a truck, when firsts come to mind
It's loads, a lot, I had a good time.
For solo sessions and short excursions,
I let my bike be my road guide.
I pick the direction,
Rubber's my selection and
Metal keeps me in protection under plastic mention.

I glide through streets, past the encaged,
Around the peddlers who say we're the slaves,
But to really take in sights and is similar to flights
And, has easier rights:
Limited or out of sight, is my rape prevention tool.
The skateboard distances rapists, especially after a blow to the back
Of their heads, then jump on it and push,
Your toosh is saved or just one step ahead.
The game between destinations has rules, some fools
Ignore them, and end in dirt.
Run a red light, like fools before, who broke the rules for one quick squirt
Of wasted gas to just get past the light, at last.
You might get hurt.

Some cars drive like me, most call them 'Granny'.
I don't pass 55, or on the right, to stay alive.
I've learned the hard way: too fast costs too much
And right side is blind side to some simple souls.
The roles on the road of life are fluid and
Reverse as fast as the flash of yellow lights
Faster than red and blue, too
The rules on the road are quite askew
And sometimes, they lend a few bends
To making amends
To few or many and it all depends
On variables.

Strong Arm the Man

[Written on 13 Jan 2008, at 7:11 A.M.]

As you stroll the scene............
There is much obscene.........
Happy endings, too..................
Or silent ones, anew.........
Many try to see....................
Each possibility...................
Be it good or bad..............
Exceeding joy or sad..........
Sand rubs the dead away.......
In time, like new, no pay............
Dis nature, Marley said.............
Exalted state in red...................
Too, yellow, green and all..............
Happy no alcohol........................
Everything on earth, we need.........
Plant in the ground, a seed...........
Like scavengers, we steal..................
A piece of heaven's field..............
Yoke what you've earned, they said......
Announce your turf instead..........
Decide the balance true.............
End heartache here and do..........
LOS ANGELES.....................

A FAVOR BY ACCepTING.,,.........,,.
All ......Flavors, as part .....,,,.......
Of ....The mix as we all ,,.........,,..
Get .... Our fix. and, ,,...,,...,...
Like ......Kool-Aid, Throw ,,...,,...,,.
Some ......Sweetness in the melt ...
Pot ....and lots of smiles IS what
You ...got! Also, dentists get a chill
................Thrill of pay
To fix and drill.

Third Graders

(Inspired by B.O.B.'s *Airplanes*, Feat. Hayley Williams, of Paramore)
[Written 20 Jun 2010]

Can we pretend
We're 3rd graders
And take our time
    To get to 1st base?

I could really use a kiss,
    Right now,
I see you here-how!
Can you deny the bow.
I give to you, each moment—
We enjoy it-we're like shooting stars

I could really use a kiss,
Right now.
Kiss, right now,
How 'bout now?

Like the vivid centerpiece
Of a flower
Bouquet, for the way you devour

All my bad thoughts/pains
They disappear!
The moment you're 15 minutes away!
From being near!

I feel the fireworks going
Off in my mind;

Goosebumps on all fronts
Yes, you're truly-a-rare-
One to find!

Prayers of gratitude & thanks
On my lips,
I pour out Praise
And love that
Our paths coexist!

I'm focused, I hope this
Time is enjoyed, by you!
Of all the others, my good-
Ness, this one's for few!

Yes, you are my moments
That pitter my heart
Pitter patter, yes, you matter
And, I've felt it from the start.

Can we pretend
We're 3rd graders-
Let's slow it down
Towards home plate?
You really got me
   Hot inside;
3 digits degrees wide
Let's build us, tonight.
I give to you, each moment-
We enjoy it—
    We're like dancing stars

I could really use a kiss,
   Right now.
Kiss, right now.
How 'bout now?!

Trifeckta Trails

[Written 09 Jun 2010]

You're everything I look for, in a mate, times 10!
I've searched high & low, still you're great, times seven.

If what I'm saying still isn't clear, a-Hem!
I love you, simply-sweetly
You are dear, and then!

Life is freer, when you see her on a team.
Life is grander, beyond grandeur, lucid dream.

Intuition, Instinct blend to fill
The gaps and spaces of climbin' that hill,

Or valley or mountain, the beach
Is the best place on earth,—
To learn and teach.

Three worlds collide,
Washed each 60 slide
Intelligent air meets
Night ground & tide

Euphoria grasped, 'til we see
AT LAST,
Our Creative Design
History in our past

The Path laced with ivy, trees, palms;
Birds fly overhead
Plane's got me singin' Psalms

Alms to the poor,
Ignored—discontent.
Proverbs galore
When you open the vent,

That has guided my life,
The Inspiring Book.

Best compass around
Bible's got me shook.

Ah, shook, shook, shook, shook, shook.
You a slave to the lame until you
Take a look,

It's sound
What's found in my
    Safety map!

So good, when disaster strikes, I take a nap!

Slap! Ah, dap! The foes close in on the gifted to win
The battle versus sin.

Stand, victory is 'round the bend.
Know your True Friend!
Find happiness within!
Jesus.

Without a doubt,
I scream and shout,
Those who've seen
A 1/10 of my clout,
Shrink n pout.

Creatures,
Critters
So-called humans;

Sharing the Trifeckta of
Earth,
Sea
And
Wind.

Love, BL!ss

Wait & Pause

[Written 21 Sept 2009]

Two things help a character grow,
According to John Tesh radio show.
Like dry grass at night, waits for dew;
Endless leaps, bounds & paths renew.
Now, building solid young souls takes time
Timid efforts lead up hills divine.

Actions echo into eternity
Never rush your given destiny
Doors will open if you strengthen
Skill of patience, go cook bacon.
  Kitchen teaches timing is everything
    In sports, I've learned milliseconds can sing;
  Like bees, sting; or that Riesling-
    Lack of control gets ya thrown out the ring
Sip your vice, if you don't play nice
May you have enough rice, perfect sized slice of
All-wheat bread, don't fake street cred.
You got to live for REAL or else you're dead.

Pretend the head is filled with air
Ask Barbie, it didn't get her anywhere
Youth may be enriched, all ways;
Take time to develop calm bays,
  Harbor many a sinking ship and
  Erupt into song, sonnet or quip

Believe me, SELF-CONTROL relates
Intricate glue appreciates
Laughter can flow when you're ready
Let loose, at times, go be steady
Sands of hour glass still pass,

Orbits move around their gas,
Revolving planets dance so free

The ballet of our moon's pretty
Handle what life throws, you're good!
Really, I've prayed, and you should
Ignore the stuff that brings you down!
Live full stamina next round!
Liverpool's brightest began sing fest
Sounds resonate on Xbox's best.

All Ways a Winner

[Written 18-21 Oct 2008]

Still goin' from the night before
This city won't sleep 'til it evens
A score or two or threesomes
Rockin' hotel walls, those wit
The balls to do it all can
Rally, give their calls, their bluffs
Announce who's tough and stuff, just
In case an argument erupts.

Nights feel cool, day's a breeze
Invited to cabanas under palm trees
Nice dreams turn bright reality,
Good times are had when I
Spend slowly. I love Vegas and
She loves me, people knowing
Of her rich history, watch
Her grow from the barren
Earth, the turf was treacherous
Just like my birth.
It rains,
It pours,
It's dry,
It's home;
To those who like to roam or
Foam-ridin' down river C
Or Hoo-ver Dam is chill
Just like Range Rovers.
Given away by slots galore
I know my score before I hit
The floor.

Break Ups Bite

[Written 22 Jan 2001]

My Body is breaking

My Mind is cracking

My self is fading

My Love is nothing
My hate is building

My soul is dying

My life is slowing

What's left?!?

Cryogenic Adjust

[Written 12 Jun 2010]

Juggling the gifts of live,
  aware souls
   Know,
and they thrive.

Nature nurtures us
  All
   Intelligence leads us
  To stall.
Now and then, a pause is
   Vital.
    Even animal kingdom knows
   Basic survival

  Ready and en guarde
Even keel on boulevards
  Night is scared of light, enter your purpose right

Carefully carefree when outpouring-good-
will REJUVENATE

Those stuck on ill food
  Mind is clear,
Conscious is well;

When environment has each
  Life-giving tell!
Tale, re-spec-table signs-

Of embracing your gifts.

Emerge and you'll find!

Free Ways, High Ways

[Written 19 Nov 2008]

Those cages enslave us and limit our view
The mazes we take make lives more askew

I Chev-Ro-Leg it and ride my bike
I still climb trees and walls with tykes.

Dad disappeared on a sleepy curve
And Godfather Joe, too, felt the swerve
The time safely tucked away with friends
Measures up, fills our cup and all depends
On how and who our life's made up

Be careful, be aware and don't erupt
Just channel your anger through a positive light
Continue to follow what you feel is right

Or break free from the pack; keep on raising your stack
And don't look back, others handle that!

This ground is my home, I pound like a gnome
Forever I roam 'til I hit the sea foam
This land is my wife
I eradicate strife
I don't grab a knife, Except for more life

Like dogs in car windows,
I love face winds
On my bike, I'm empowered to still chase Linds
We shot each other that flashy look
And sooner or later, she'll read my book

That I wrote to her and all the rest.

The ones, I feel exude the best.

I share my experiences,
I care to spread knowledge,

The womyn in my presence could all use college.

It may not matter the subject you choose
So long as your heart, mind and soul do not lose!

The yearning to prosper, to earn, to burn,
Keep hope alive
And continue to churn.
Keep on truckin', keep rollin' on;
Do not dwell on those who-ask-you to move on!

   Move on! If they disrespect

   Go on out, if they neglect
   If you're not in their top 3

   Then how much are you really
   Gonna be part of their history,

   Makin' amends, while losin' glee?
   Misery in company or happiness alone
   Try to find your balance, then you'll feel at home.

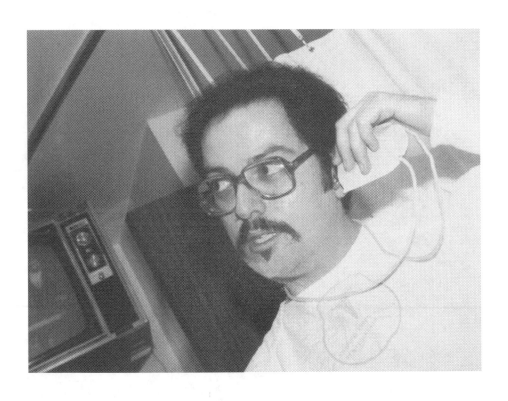

Good to Know

[Written 13 Jun 2008]

God, when I'm good, guide me through life.

Some may not understand, but that's why there's strife . . .
All my needs are provided,
And my wants aren't one-sided.

Life has its up and downs.
Sometimes, it's full of clowns.
I know one thing, though, I'm safe & sound.
My Lord bats my enemies away with one round.

Pretending as a possum prevents strife soakin' in,
When it hits the fan, either I lose or I win.

The lesson of experience continually grows
My branches; expanding, like my hand & it knows

Sometimes, love needs shade
At times, just a ray but,
Remember, excess or lack of sun, then, you'll pay,

As well as the others involved in your love
We know rain comes from cotton balls above
In our sky, the horizon hides
Don't know why & still she rides

Our earth without remorse
Her view's a steady course

Give and take,
Balance is met
Dry and dusty,
Cool and wet

A lil' of both nourishes souls
Contained on the mountain or in the rolls,
Of hills, valleys, rivers, lakes;
My knowledge has been built upon mistakes.

Heart Saver

[Written 12 Jun 2010]

I only wanna make, make
And unbreak your heart!

They call me heart saver
Sweet like a life saver
Well-rounded in my Saviour

Creator of bees' knees
Author of growin' grass an' trees

Nothing can separate us
From His Love,
    It nurtures & grows

I only wish to take, take
Away all your pains

I'm in it for the long haul
Some say that's insane
Open your soul to taste, taste
What goodness there is—

I've felt the full potential
Love is all there is—

Open your mind, more and ease
Will embrace your core
Full throttle now-round,
You'll see what's
    In store.

I Can't Complain

[Written 11 Jun 2010]

Girls get at me!
Gosh, they're friendly!
Confidence, smooth talk
Aplenty . . .
Back rubs, soft-shoves &—
Goosebumps—too many . . .

Lovin' 'em all,
Havin' a ball,
As we
Enjoy our company,

The girls get at me,
Gosh, they pushy,
One more
Straw & I
Might get mushy,
Tushy grabs
Won't cease,
Release the tension,
    I'm at peace.

Lord's Care Everywhere

[Written 10 April 2010]

Luscious green, out the window of the terminal.
This must be Eire-re,
But it feels like Missouri.

Gray skies lurk like Kansas City,
Did when last I left the past.
Behind
My steps, the shadows depth

Ebbs and flows, the moon, aglow
Light pours beneath me, and fills me through.

A day and night have passed,
The sun warms me to the core!
All the ends of the earth, I'll explore.

Some do through books, some meet the crooks
That shook the pocketbooks
Of those on foot.

They fair, well, to leave all
Behind, some stare instead of the
Vine,
Branch,
Grasp of truth,
Know the sleuth
Who slips by you.
Unaware targets of a thief,
Pay attention!
Don't blow away like a leaf!

Belfast is around the corner
Portsmouth is down that way
Edinburgh has plenty students
Oslo is in Norway.

Lubeck and Hamburg have history.
Helsinki rhymes with slinky and there's Napoli!

Roma, Marseille and Palermo,
    Let's go!
Athinai, Thessaloniki, Istanbul, Cairo.

Europe's finest, London & Glasgow,
Stockholm has seen my letters
Since two decades ago!

Kobenhavn, water galore!
Berlin, Warszawa, Harlinger, whoa!

Ya gotta visit Rotterdam and Pamplona!
Bayonne, Le Havre, Lisboa,
Madrid, Gibraltar!

I love Galway and Dublin,
Everything in between
    And all around.

It feels good to move
Around the cities
And each feels like home,
Los Angeles and
San Francisco,
Fiji,
Maui,
My home,
Our land.

My Bush

[Written end of Jun 2010]

My bush is perfectly shaped; your bush appears attacked by apes.
My bush flowers every hour. Your bush flowered last before fell the twin
    towers.
My bush is lush greenery. Your bush has two leaves and is scraggily.
My bush spirals through the roof. Your bush looks like it's missin' a tooth.
My bush's been growing since 2000 B.C.; your bush still has recent toddler
    history.
My bush roams wild 'n free. Your bush is in and out of custody.
My bush can pull 2 sheaves of wheat. Your bush sees Jack with the EBT.

My bush never DUI. Your bush so sad, it cries and lies.
My bush has won awards. Your bush keeps getting cut back with swords.
My bush is truly a rare breed; your bush sells for 2 cents a seed.
My bush sits next to Kobe; your bush gets smashed by paparazzi!

    So many bushes
Eclectic mix
Follow your heart true
Forget your fix and
Politics should study
Game plans.
Forefathers before took care
Of fellow man

And woah, man! When
You work on your tan
Don't overdue it,
Prevent that cancer scan
From invading
A good day.
Take care of what counts
Love your neighbors, today

Those bushes blow out
Amounts
of what
Sustains our lungs to pull—
the earth's lines
Have shown—falls, fast
The fool

My bush lasts eons of lifetimes
Your bush rarely gets on primetime

Outside Sometime

[Written 11 Aug 2009]

Agoraphobes need not apply
And, homophobes, ask yourself why?!
I'm free to be! How God loves me!
My love increases 'bout daily.

When on a date, I don't need wine
I'd like to go outside, sometime
Let's hike the mount, or bike the coast.
A camping trip, marshmallow roast!

The beauty, found within nature

Calms the wayward mind and heart.

My soul regainin' its stature,

Grows along the still waters part.

You wanna see me doing fine?
Let's take a walk outside, sometime
I'll carry you, you can lift me up!
I love you, dear. I'll back you up!

American Grrrl

(Inspired by Estelle's *American Boy*)
[Written 2008]

[Boi] You know, girl, we love the same games,
Time after time, we've played them
Rockin' at pool halls to anthems
Keepin' it sane like we got them
I've learned all about how we're the same
Once lame, sometimes tame
I love you, girl, the same
You are my favorite American Grrrl.

[Boi] I'll take you on a trip, I wanna go somewhere
There's many spots to show you just how much I care.
I really want to get busy with you
I'll be your Tom Tom Boi

[Grrrl] You asked me what I've learned from you, I paused to count the ways
Then, lost count, knew I'z hooked without a single doubt.
That smile was for, you've evened the score,
I'm lost without you, human compass, get me home . . .
Our temporary spot to chill, explore and so much more
Let's stop in Devore. I'm your one American Grrrl.

[Boi] I'll take you on a trip, I'd like to go somewhere.
Nashville has my roots, though Ackland has some flair
Ibiza is nice, Thailand has good rice
I'll be your Tom Tom Boi

[Grrrl] Dah Dah Dah Dee Dum, Dah Dah Dah Dee Dum, Dan Dah Dee
Dee Dam!

[Boi] I'll be your Tom Tom Boi
She said, Bois don't usually come this good
From what I've understood, they all about one thing.
I retorted, while I sing, get ready for anything.

[Grrrl] You're an international joy
[Boi] I'll be your amazing chew toy
[Grrrl] You'll be with me, eternally, and more
[Boi] I'll be there to help you destroy,
Anything in your path and more
[Grrrl] Heal me and more, release me,
Don't store your joy;
Don't hold back, I got your back, Tom Tom Boi

[Grrrl&Boi] We'll head out on a trip, Yes, we will get us there,
Just close our eyes and spin the globe
Let's see what's where, so long as you're there
The world, I will share
You are my American Boi/Grrrl.

[Boi] I love you, you're stealth, let's pour out our wealth
For those who lack how to deposit in the bank of love, that skill
Some back,
Like docs, crocs and smocks, without attacks
From unknown force, which destroys steady course.
I love you, now, let's check on our horse,
Then ride no remorse. Where to, hun?

Grrrl] Spain has lots of spice
[Boi] In France, they cannot see
[Grrrl&Boi] Paparazzi won't find us
[Grrrl] It's just you and me
[Boi] I've yet to go to Mardi Gras
[Grrrl] In New Orleans, let's go!
[Grrrl&Boi] We'll chill on coasts of Africa
[Boi] Find new species in Calcutta
[Grrrl] Drift off to Manila, visit Saigon & Lisboa.
Rotterdam is calling, Vanuatu, too.
[Boi] Let's relax down under, or hear Alabama thunder
How 'bout stroll on the Great Wall of China
Then dance in Russia's grand halls
I'll catch ya if you fall, I'm loving Amsterdam, don't stall
Tell me you are down for it, all, American Grrrl.
[Grrrl] I am, let's scram
I will, let's chill
I do, oh, boo
[Grrrl&Boi] I do love you.

[Boi&Grrrl] We'll head out on a trip, any way's fine with me
Diversity's our friend
Let's sail the shining sea.
We really be down
For all that's around
We're an international joy!
[Boi]You're my American Grrrl
[Grrrl] You're my Tom Tom Boi

Care in a Day

[Written 04 Oct 2008]

Anger, guilt and jealousy may
Disrespect your self.

The less a child senses panic,
The less they will feel panic.
Pain and suffering cease.
Bliss, joy and peace increase.

Frustration, stress and worry, I place
Upon a shelf   They helped me
Grow and know my pace
In hills, valleys and straights

I used insights from history
Of those who I felt were great

That Simpson showed same day, wrong
Crime: we care more of material
Than when a life's on the line.

When we know our role
It's easier to let someone patrol.
It may not matter who has control
So long as destination is clear, a go.
One way, many perspectives on how to grow
Sun, water, sustenance and blooms will show.

Dearest Friend,

[Written June of 2008]

I love you, at no cost.
I saw you alone and a lil' lost,
    And wondered why you cry.
I cry in crowds where I am not high,
Not on drugs, because you taught me that those
Get you nowhere safe,
I'm aware of that,
    I suppose.
You say that you're blue
I got news for you
My sad tears dried when
Applied my motto.
No, unlike you, it's not lotto,
I've been to an amazing grotto
As I got a different view
    In your sister's auto.
If you're down and out
I'll share a route
That in my life
  Left little doubt.
Sometimes, our path gets
Murky, rough.
And, yes, it strengthens, yes, it's tough.

But ever, if you've lost your
Map, make a new one or take a nap.
Then, gaze at what's repped
And do it high!
By tree,
Building
    Or mountain top, here's why:
   Your perspective is one of three;
   A microscope
   And telescope will tell thee
The small and big details
That may stand out in your mind,
Out in your hand
Believe me, this, on sand
Or any land
To navigate, safely, you need
Two hands
One from you and one from the stands
Of those who support you,
Those who care or anyone
Who offers, to be there.

Freestyle Flow to tune of "Have I the Right?"

[Written 2 Dec 2010]

Have I the right to kiss you?
You do know THAT I'd miss you
What did I do?
What have I done wrong?

I sing my relief song, now.
You know me, better than any gal,
I know—don't you show me
How much care
There could be, oh be-HAVE!
I started
Patching, change my ways
That don't work, to show
My love's sincere.

Oh, please! Put down the beer,
And hear, me out—
There's more than one perspective
On our routes
Twenty may come to the surface
Realness and worth may hurt this
Wall, you-u've built!
Let love embrace your being
Live life full color, meaning—

Fun-filled times~~~
Galore, and through every door,
Girl, you'll find!
The path of least resistance
May shatter in an instance.

Choices, educated
Circumstances, weighted
Changing the sails of our success

Winds-hook, baited
Chasing wind like thunder
Chases light, asunder

Knowing half the battle
Actions speak so louder

Gracious Givings

[Written 4 Sept 2010]

Body needs: rejuvenation
Mind is clear and alert
Spirit, lifted! Thanks, Our Savior!
Souls are cared in Him since birth

And, beyond, before there were;
Doors to open, leave ajar . . .
Life advances, we are sure . . .
Of so little, yet a star—shone down
So Eastern leaders;
Could find & worship The King!

Israel's King David spoke of
Him, that's why he danced,
And sing, sing, sing
We make music into heaven.
I do be-lieve. Yes,
His Word does give us
Answers! OH, I praise His Name

I do proclaim the Kingdom
Of Kingdoms,
Ruled by the Prince of Peace
Is what I'm seeking, first
Let heaven and nature sing!
Matt 6:33 tells of His
Righteousness. He is just.
In Him, I trust. I give
My best! Put in my ALL!
Endure the test,
hop over the hurdles,
Smooth over speed bumps,
break down barriers,
Tear down walls,
Brick by brick,
overcome stalls
Chug through thick, lick them, all!
We stand tall,
Go, marching, on—
Follow the battle call!

The Lord reigns, forever
Victory, ahead
The children of God, with love, are led.

Here, Mama

[Written 07 Jan 2008]

Feelin' alright, despite the fight
Inside my mighty mind. I find
That the plight of being right
Or feelin' wrong or wronged, for so long,
Mourning decay, dismay
Discontent from heaven-sent.

I repent and relentlessly
Aim to maintain
The skinny and narrow, like Pharaoh
Or follow the side lines through the thick,
Past the wide open countryside,
I watch the tide and ride.
To coincide, I do confide
All that I hide behind no lies or enemy lines.

I keep it sweet and on the beat,
Though sometimes near, when music's clear
To somewhat sear the inner ear
Is hurtin' dear, so speak up, true. I can't hear you.

My Uncle Sam gave jobs so grand,
I hurt my hand and lost my voice,
Though a fine choice
I chose to hoist above the moist
Tinge of defeat, to those repeating
History, a flag of white may or not right,
Those lacking sight
Attack and stand
Between the grand
Task here, at hand.
I land
With a thud
Through mucky crud

I fall to rise and realize
That nothing here can cease to lie. I like to pry
When those get wry with how I cry.
It's just release, how I get peace
Inside my heart,
Because it starts
There and ends there.

In Love After

[Written 10 Jul 2008]

You look so good above
You still show your love
I see you in a dove
Hope comes like a soft shove

Into outer space, I used to look
A book or two, did have me shook
Great volumes hit me in my head
Slightly scrambled, though not dead

I'm aware of your care
Why else would you share?
Your jeans fit mc right
Prince said, "Outta sight"

In my dream, we all laugh
In my mind, I need a bath
Keep on truckin' like Dead Heads
I'm homeless with many beds

Neglect comes from blind
Abuse comes from wine.

Lower Shiver

[Written 12 & 17 Dec 2008]

Stamina, I'm a swimmer.
Ups, yes, I deliver
Amazin', sparkin' quiver
Lurkin' before your dinner

Wide awake, I give,
I can't take, I
Love for Heaven's sake
And yes, Oh's
I make. Loyal, when
Called and I'll
Pause when stalled
By manipulative
Heart-soul-mind, I true live

Estates receive care and they
Shine well aware of the reason
I stare. Yes, I have a good pair!

Time is mine as I continue to shine
Announce that she's fine and
Tumble away from swine that you
Exhaustedly sent. Look, girl, I'm
Not bent.
Your maturity must have
Been lent
To another, so repent.

My Name's Crazy-Peace, Love, Unity and Respect a.k.a. MNC-PLUR

(Inspired by Slim Shady's song)
[Written 13 Jun 2008]

I'm a tomboi. Yes, I'm a real joy
All you unhonest ladies, please don't destroy (me)
So, won't the real tombois
Please, get up,
Please, stand up!
Please, stand up.

Now, the bois of the world
Some big, some small;
Some do give and many stand tall.

I've seen ya before, in the hall, at school;
We may, over the same prize, had a duel,
Or at some cool club, while we actin' the fool.
And, don't ya dare drool, 'cause I'm already cool.

I got some news for you and yours
I've finished some tests and got high scores
Since you're like a brother
Our Mother earth
Tells me she's seeing that another one
Has infiltrated our turf

It's killin' our dirt.
It lessens our squirt and it has even
Tainted what quenches our thirst

And, if we sit here, do nothing,
It's gonna get worse

There's many solutions, but the problems are blurry
Squirrels run off in a hurry;
Even bums, for food, scurry.

We, as a family, should change our ways
And, it pays, in the end, so our sons pave the way
To glory and honor, if we set them right,
Give them sight to some plight,
Hopefully,
Shed some light,
On the way to our roots becoming solid

We can't kid anymore
This is our home, so bid,
Blow the lid off what you THINK you can do.
It's true, the sky's the limit
And, the key's inside you.

And, if you can listen to a heart beat,
I can tell ya what's true,
I can share something neat.
Our family tree of hip hop
Is like a rose from concrete
The beat, yes, it's sweet and it makes
Me complete, but beat
Moves the ground and our enemy is near
And our clan must survive,
For the winter is here.

L.A. County began my roots
Rotten oranges nourished under my boots

I leaned to one hip,
Took a wind up to throw with one rock a skip
Across nothing to go and a figurative touch
Has done so much,
My fans understand
What keeps me going and such.

Path to What?

[Written at 4:19 PM, on 27 Feb 2008]

Coincidence, or not, all that I've sought
Rains down on me, slicks, my hair like the licks;
I cry out in pain, the weak go insane;
Seems strength from within, and lacking in sin;

Takes some of the force from the ungifted horse;
In my mind sits this: thoughts of constant bliss;
Numbs the fractures and aches
And from my heart, it makes

Mounds of resisting joy
Onward to foil their ploy
Rally the troops, I've found a map
Aware of the scare that it's a trap

Legions before have failed and fell
Each short of their goal they know so well
See something new, greed ain't only way
Care and honor HELPS one THRIVE in a day

And that power trip's more like an acid trip
Lend a hand, don't demand, or you just might slip
Down a path with, less routes,
Ending dead in roundabouts

Reaching nowhere,
Or worse, this verse, unrehearsed;
Now, go follow the cursed, or make your own.

 With Love,
  "BL!ss"
 Cristina M. Calderon

Somebody From Compton Loved Me

[Written May 7, 2008; At 9:15 A.M.]

Well, I'm not sure from where she came
I asked before, but thought it lame
For, you see, the raising grew
Toward the light but darkness knew

Away from Compton she flew the nest
Neglecting no one, except herself
Determined to shine above the rest
Can't see success when you don't give best

Like country songs, she lost it all
Each day I cry, feeling her fall
Aware it's her path, never mine
Now, that's some confidence and you will find

I'm doing fine, I've got my own
I'm living good, despite the bills
There's death, each corner, I do see
It's is not yet, my reality

So simmer down, wait 'til you boil
Or rush it and feel the spoil
Know where your land is and toil
When the timing's there to foil

Evil lurks and so do snakes
Good can come from our mistakes

Swim Deep

[Written at 1:30 P.M., on 15 Jun 2007]

Why do we rely on metal or even plastic?
Each day we find ways around nature
And she forgives us every single time
Pointing fingers at us not
Obviously but obliviously
Now, how can we ignore our vessel through
Space and time and all around us

Pounding on our mother the poor ground
Realizes that it's being crushed
Overpopulation of the tired nations
Trying to maintain peace and
Every one of us sees the signs
Calculated and predicted
Time's almost up for our existence

Determined souls control the fate
Each day I try to hesitate
Sustain my heart and try to be
Together in this life
Really, truly finding ways to be
Onward to my
Young journey to the moon and sun, the stars have won.

'Til Parts Fall Off

[Written 11 Jul 2008]

You asked 'til when
I thought 'til infinity
Who didn't believe
My love philosophy?

Your friends don't count
But your family may know
I'll show you how
Our relationship can grow

'Til parts fall off
I'll be for you
'Til parts just rot
I'll love you, true
If any stop, my motive's
Clear, until they
Stop to have a beer

You've lost control before
On booze. I've had a hold,
Your enemies lose.
Remember, I lost guts,
Lost glory. I still stand
For you, so there's my story

Plain and true, just like you asked
And only you can kiss my past.

Turn Over A New

[Written 2 Mar 1998]

Deep within, burning still

The light will go

Out no more, noon

Comes I'm undone

Fresh as the morn dew

I change also

But not until

Turn I the leaf.

Untitled

[Written 21 Aug 2008]

Young Justin opens the door, one
Day and to his surprise,
Shock and dismay,
His neighbor trembled before his eyes,
And before he could even realize,
She collapsed there, at his stoop.

In tears, she screamed,
"Damn my years and fcuk those beers."
He picked her up, amongst the sobs
She buried herself like a slob
Into his shoulder, her problems resolved.
A warm support helped all involved.

Yankee Dams

[Written 1 Jun 2008]

I wanna collaborate, not cohabitate
Like I told you before, I don't wanna date
I see ya sit & wait, I hear ya
Say I'm Kate, but I'm carin'
To be sharing with my own chose mate.

You come at me with this,
You get at me with that.
I see your face, sometimes, and
All I see's a rat

I've tripped, fell and bleed
Just like you, and your seed
I don't need, yet, so back off & take heed.

I've seen, felt & heard nearly every story.
You're boring, at times,
And, so sounds my glory
I'm done with the gory details, for now
'Cause, well, it's time for chow & I don't see how

You can watch my back as you stare at my front
And, don't front what you know you don't even got.
I've sought for some before,
Yes, I've evened the score.
I've opened up
Some amazing doors
And, I've shown you the pictures,
Remember my MySpace
Page after page
Of my travels through time, space

And I never make haste
'Cause I waste nothing
On earth, we just be reusing our old space

And, I'll tell you, again,
I want nothing from you.
Your answer for that question, why?
Well, like I told you:
I've seen ya face before, though
The time was uncertain

One thing I remember.
I was one who was hurtin'.

The stains left by someone similar
I cry every night, wash it down with vinegar
Many whom I love have stained
Every inch of the base of my heart
And they think it's a pinch.
I say it's a cinch, so they don't give an inch
Now, I'm left with nothing
Or I could just snitch, but
Carrying weight just ain't my thing
And my one love to sing, well,
Ghouls would say, with one wing
Even small ones go far, either by bus or by car
Or by starring in a flick wit utopian bliss
Where one kisses one or two or another
'til interrupted by some sister or brother
Comes in with a gun, that ain't right under my sun
So, understand this, you lost me when I requested
Presence in your heart
So, your silence has set me apart

And, I've left to start on the ladder between
You and me, so you could hear me sing
Phatter beats, bolder blends
But, all of that won't matter
If you don't have a lil' patience
This skill takes chatter & time
And, I've tried to make it easier
So, here's my rhyme, decipher, if you want to, but I'm still on time,
No mo mo's in the world make me stop on a dime, except
Animals, kids & those not out doing crime, 'cause

I'm so sick of the grime and if you hand me a lime,
At least my drink's doing fine. And, you'll see in due time,
I'm fine & have been sippin' on great wine, with the prime
Cuts accompanied by choice bounty the county rewards those
Who help not hurt the land
Some of the easiest lessons are the hardest to learn
But, like Faith Hill said, I want you to BURN, 'cause if I don't
See your candle, then, I might not make the turn
And, some lessons, only once we learn.

Been There, Won That

[Written 07 Jan 2010]

Cars swerve by, I feel the rush
Girls hit girls, I see the lush
Dogs smell dogs and bark at bad
Kids cry "Kid, why are you sad?"

    Situations call for wisdom
    Innocent bystander victim
    Runs for cover, run for time
    Sweet how Forrest ran so fine

Movies show the silver lining;
Screens may stop
the constant whining—
Of lost souls, downtrodden ones;-
Scared to reach out, helpful guns,-
With elbow grease
can make ill ease
Your arms to hug spark, evil cease—
To bring you down!, stand up tall

Last round for round
   right here or mall
Or mission, wishin' bright tomorrow
Love the present, end your sorrow.
Hike or bike or help a tyke
Love your neighbor,
   foe or dyke!
Follow inspiring leaders on,
Hit that timid, large peace gong—
I pray for guidance, win awards,
Ace the tests by word or swords.
God watches over daughter, BL!ss
The morning dew is nature's kiss,
Upon the earth the burden lifts.
Snowboard-skate-surf the many gifts,
We sometimes take for granted, here.
I love the Lord, He protects and is near.
Lift my all to Our God, my hearts' sincere.

The Lord is my Shepherd;
He eradicates fear
Been there, won that
I thank the Savior
Warrior & Poet—how's that to savor?

Careful, Calculated

[Written 27 Jun 2010]

Step one, smile
Step two, hug a few.
Step three, share.
Friendships last through
Tender, loving care

Step four, chill. Step five, a live.
Step six comes natural, dance 'n jive.
Step seven, essential to thrive,
Prayer, reflection.

Courage to go on,
When all seem to give up . . .
Know the detection of those
Soon to erupt.

Peace, love and happiness
Thrive in the life of
Those givin' up strife up to
The Lord, who cuts down
Our enemies
With His Word.

Delicate Souls

[Written 11 Oct, 2000]

Fluttering in my stomach
The butterflies won't cease
I feel the need to panic
But, somehow, I'm at ease.

Great comfort unsurpassed, so free
Bestowed on me unexplained
Her reasons why our unity
No answer, no one was blamed

With great caution, I must use
My senses, she won't leave
Me, I cannot again lose
Or I'll lose my belief

In finding what I need to live
The right seed that time will sow
Maybe if all my heart I give
My life will begin with NOW.

Friendly Vent, Essay on Told Ya So

[Written Tuesday afternoon, May 01, 2007, by Cris Bliss]

Why is it that girls run into my arms when they are hurt by another? I do my best to comfort them and not speak negatively about the situation at all, even when it was the other person who did something awful, like, say cheating. The girls usually cry and tell me how horrible the relationship was in the first place . . . "She was too possessive" "She didn't like my friends" "We didn't have a lot in common, other than compatibility in the bedroom (which I don't need to know, especially if I was once compatible, with the distraught girl, in the bedroom!)" "I could never bring the (lying, cheating) lover home to Mom" . . . etc.

Darn, I do my best to let them know it's best to move on. When you're in a situation like that, where you have to compromise constantly . . . isn't it best to CUT YOUR LOSSES and find another lover??? I've given this advice to many. Call me a relationship counselor, if you may. Those who have stuck with my advice eventually got over the lover who was caught cheating or lying. I know I couldn't live with myself accepting a lying, cheating partner. I have better standards than that. I try to comfort my friend, the hurt girl and encourage her to raise her standards, even just a little bit. That seems to be the best advice, when followed. My friends, who listen to me, find someone or something else to preoccupy their time and life is good, again. When the girl goes back to the possessive lover, the lover tends to get more possessive and then more negative occurrences happen and then they are calling me YET AGAIN to complain, cry and vent about a lover with which they knew they shouldn't get back involved with.

Yeah, I've heard many scenarios played out, and I've seen some end up violent. I have had to put myself in danger to break up a fighting couple . . . I guess that comes with the territory. Cris Bliss, here trying to help you remain in bliss, be it to give relationship counseling or mere advice, I'm always here for the girls . . . anytime you need me, I'll be here. Just please listen to my time-honored advice or I will be a little disappointed when you come back at me with the same old problems.

Grandmas, Don't Let Your Babies

[Written 28 Jun 2008, inspired by
Willie Nelson's "Mamas, Don't Let Your Babies]

Grandma, I didn't listen to Mama and grew up
A cowboi
She told me, 'Don't do it', I'd die alone
And sing songs all about it, on stages, in phones.

From early on, my days on the playground of life,
Were playing cowboys and engines, not doctor and wife.
G.I. Joe appealed to me more than Barbie baloney
Although, with other girls, I did share love of ponies.

Grandma, I didn't listen to Papa, I grew up
A cowboi
He showed fine examples of what I could be
Scientists and wrench drivers sound so good, to me.

I tried my hand at soldiering, then corporate America.
Both shot me down, don't know if my gender or being brown,
Led to hurting and cussing' 'em out.

Grandmas, don't let your babies
Grow up, to be cowboys, (or tombois, for that matter!)
I do love my guitar and ride in ol' trucks
I lost all my money to docs, lawyers and such!

Following dreams to be
On film, record and TV came to fruition.
Now, I'm wishin' I didn't share my dreams
With those I thought loved me and my mission.

They now shoot me down
And it's hurts worse than my frown.
Acknowledge, still, my love for all
That I've met around!

Grandma, I listened to you
And grew up how I wanted.
My dreams may get shattered,
Crushed or delayed,
But new ones arise
    And blossom with the day!

I love all your wisdom you passed on to me,
Be it through words, timed silence or your genes.

Hurt, Less

[Written 21-22 Sept 2009, inspired by
Johnny Cash's rendition of NIN's Hurt]

The hurt from yesterday
Is stinging less and less
I love a year and a day,
And give my very best.

I won't let you down,
You have healed my hurt!
I am still, before you,
Calmed with full comfort.

The candle of our love, glows steady
In the wind.
My feelings, so above; quite long ago, begin

Each heart-skipped moment seared,
Into soul memory. You have changed me
So, that I can hardly breathe.

Like the doe panting, for refreshing sip
I breathe You full in, and my head I dip

Kings before agree, You are number One
Each intricate soul lives or dies half or whole

Ask me anything! For you, I do live
Some do know the grasp, of Your love and
How giv-ING fills the holes, yes,
Every gap; Your Word is so clearly
Life's safety map. If I stopped to list,
Forever, I would go, Your endless Grace
Is the everlasting glow! This
World shows-all-Your-Love.
Enamored, yes, I am; You reign
And Heaven above Holds us dear;
(We) Raise our hand!

In the Name of . . . ?

[Written 07 Nov 2007]

Yennnn! I am getting tired of men;
    They rape and pillage where I've been.
    I laugh, and cry to hide my side
    But patience is wearing thin . . .

    Do I ask for fists to face?
    Am I really a disgrace?
    My voice, unwavering, a waste?
    Announce no winners in this race?

    Glued to tv's telling lies
    Enthralled in nothing's a surprise
    Determined ones all in disguise
    Go between here and the skies.

    On battlefield, earth
    Omnipotent by birth
    Do not stand in my way, for
    Someone else collects my pay.

Mic "Hoe" Idol

A ganja farmer

His story, told in song (Inspired by Sean Kingston's *Beautiful Girls*)
[Saturday, August 25, 2007]

Dang all these beautiful bois, they only wanna do you dirt, they'll have you homicidal, homicidal when they kick you o-ver.

It started in the town where you're allowed to make a sound
And it won't get back to your home ground, unless your name is Paris or Britney.
If you do it properly, like what you learned from history
that one coke princess you met in rehab, see. The one, the one looking like Lindsay, the one from grade school, what a darn fool.

Dang all these beautiful bois, they only wanna do you hurt, they'll have you homicidal, homicidal when they kick you un-der.

Your average tomboi would try to destroy the other competition to get your joy, the one who didn't bring the coca. It seems in my playground, here, the beer removes fear. And if your demons are severe
then they try to smear your nose with candy,
from the wrong side of the tracks.
Your mom warned us, gee,
that almost very surely,
the drugs and ways would overtake ya needs
til ya drop to ya knees
and pray about the things
that keep ya breathin, keep ya breathin'!

Dang all these beautiful bois, they only wanna do you mean, they'll have you homicidal, homicidal throwin' punches, feelin' lean.

Now, when others attack you when no one's got your back, ya try your best to lack the stamina or knowledge of the fight, the pointless quarrel, at hand.
If they forcin' ya to flex while your mommy says you're best
but you can't quite seem to pass the darn test
Ya run, but there's no more doors to open.
If you look harder, you'll see,
the one in the mirror maybe
may show you another
To vent your wrath
At
The difficult crossroads, at hand.

My Roots, Exposed

[Written 14 Jun 2008]

I'm bleeding for unknown reasons
I noticed the small cut, after some
Blood dried
It doesn't hurt as much as the pain in my side,
But the scope of it
Is a mile wide.

Butterflies in my belly
   Tell me
Life still has me

I sting like a bee, if you try to stand next to me
Without first
giving dues or saluting or smoke.

Remember, a pirate on land is like a punch-line-missing joke.

If I'm missing the glue
That keeps me to earth
I don't need it from you,
For I'm already birthed
   and bathe
Had time with slaves and pigs,
And, saved something,
For you and your kids.

Your share of the booty
Comes after we dap,
Clap, or talk
How 'bout let's make a rap?

Smoke signals from my ancestors
Tell me you're true
And the sky
In my eye says the world is half blue

The green and brown other half,
Tainted with white
Looks better with flowers bathed in light

And, a myriad of murals enlightens us, too
I've made my own flag, how 'bout you?

Patience of a Saint

[Written 13 Oct 2010]

Feeling hunger
    Spare change, still, to beggars
Aching thirst
    Split the bounty-like tax county

Battered, beaten, broken
    Help each other get that
      Victory Ring

Even at the lowest, we
    Sing to the Highest!
      The greatest win!
    Trust In Him!
      Who removes sin!

Zoso: made whole
  So-so feelings, no more.

Refined through fire like our
Earth's rare treasures—
Patience of a Saint
God gives the full measure.

So True

[Written 10 July 2007 At 9:05 p.m.]

Stay away from dirty boys and fags, mmm-kay?
Cause it seems like AIDS is here to stay, no way!

Stand up tall and Ms. Right may appear in sight
Shoulders back so itty bitty's shine in light

All is due to you
When the truth shines through
Caring, loving soul
Full of self-control
Love is fresh, anew
Your spirit, so true.

Helping other kindred souls
Takes the halves, making wholes.
Dig deep to find the better
Treasures of mother EARTH.

Fill hearths with songs and dancing
Shake chimneys 'til soot falls
Follow your heart among this
Darkness presents sun's call.

Spanky's Mom

(Inspired by the song, *Stacey's Mom*, by Fountains of Wayne)
[Written 2 Jul 2010]

Spanky's Mom has got it goin' on (x4)

Spanky, would ya wipe your drool (wipe your drool)
Your Mom is hott! I'm no fool (but I too, drool)
Did ya tell her that I love her quite a bit (quite a bit)
Is she aware that she's beyond 5 star tip (5 star tip)

You know, I'm ready to handle what life throws me
So, throw yourself, fully, honey, into me!

Spanky's Mom has got it goin' on
Since start of year, clearly, hits the right gong
Spanky, can't you tell, that I wish to do her well
I hope that you don't mind that I'm in love with Spanky's Mom

Spanky's Mom has got it goin' on (x2)

Spanky, do you think I stand a chance (stand a chance)
If I asked your Mom, to the local dance? (Salsa or hip hop dance)
She really drives me crazy, FYC can't compare (none can compare)
Like INXS sang, "I need you, tonight"! My Dear (Yes, my Dear!)

And I don't think that she'd be mad at me
If I told her she has a beautiful body.
She can hold it against me

Spanky's Mom has got it goin' on
She's what I crave, ooh, I've waited soo long
Spanky, would you please, put in a good word for me
She sparks in me a song
Wow, I'm in love with Spanky's Mom

Spanky's Mom has got it goin' on
Can't ask for more, she's better than beer pong
Spanky, let's unite on making this Queen feel right
Sparks go off, all along, and oh oh
(Sparks go off, all along)
I'm in love with (Spanky's Mom oh oh)
(Spanky's Mom oh oh)
I'm in love with Spanky's Mom!

Sweetly Opened Eyes

[Written 17 Dec 2008]

Atop the slide I strived to be,
The ladder there was quite easy,
'Til I got pushed, my poor toosh squooshed
At least, land I not on the bush
With thorns which scorns the wayward path
I laugh; cry 'til I fill a bath
The wrath of me, few seldom see
I swim from sea to windy sea
Don't approach me silent, stealth
I got my wealth & here's to health

Like Heath, I looked through eyes of knights
The whites of those inclined to fights
I avoid, avert, and live
For my love, my heart I give

Announce your presence,
Friend or foe
Or plain don't know which way to go.
I strike first, ask questions later
Got femmes galore no masturbate
Or have to jump another soul
I got control, please know your role

Because revenge is never mine.
Legions attack, appear as swine
I lead in Truth; I'm doin' fine.
Respectin' those who toast with wine
Or beer or booze
Or blunts or glitches
Hittin' switches or earnin' them britches!
Who wears the pants in yours?
Who the heck's keepin' scores?
Why stick with all the bores?
How could you just ignore?

The "I'm not touching you" game is lame
Why ask for it, then cry and blame?
Your ill-thought acts may bring you shame
Don't push me, yo, I'm nice and tame.

Take Time

[Written 16th Nov 2007]

This bridge I'm on
May crumble in the quake
Instead of worry comin'
I wake and bake a cake

Too little time to give regar-ds
To ill thoughts deep down dark boulevards

I may be swimmin' against the re-st
In time, they'll see, I'm still the best

Time's not wasted when after a goal
And I don't need you to make me whole
Killin' time is what I do And I make time to see you through
Every day I'm not with yo-u, just fills my head with you-know-who

My life is sweet when you fill me up
My plate looks good as I lift my cup
Every thing you do for me, I se-e
Exactly right here is where I want to be.

You wash my clothes
You wash my ass (donkey)
And do the dishes when I don't ask
You build me up
You fill me up
With the good lovin' few womyn
    Know to give up!

I get down when we boogie
Remember the boogie?
You laugh every time
I do the boot scootin' boogie!

This bridge I'm on
May crumble in the quake
Instead of worry comin'
I wake and bake a cake,
For you, My Love.

This One's A Keeper

[Written 12 Nov 2008, inspired by a Reba McEntire song]

I'll be here,
When ol' dead beats
Finally disappear
From your perfect face
I'll always have a place
For you, even your kids
Can come, too
I'll be there,
For you.

I'm not through
I've seen the future, it's with you
And more blue skies
Than you'd imagine
Like John, here's my mansion,
Rich in knowledge
And expansion
With more experience
Than Hanson's.

Top Notch Week

[Written 28 Dec 2009 & 13 Jan 2010]

Was free styling, as the sun
    set in the sky.
I have a habit of
    answering why—
Too much information,
Invades our nation,
Schooled, played a fool,
Charged to the top with my team-
Livin' life, without strife—everything is supreme.

Dreams realized as my eyes on da prize—
Toastin' with won wise
Materialize

The inevitable
Gravity is a variable,
The respectable, fine spectacle
Know the detectable
To fit the bill, ride the thrill
Aware, prepare for Jill or Jack,
It's white, it's black
You may take a step back,
Learn pause before attack,

The stubborn'll come around,
It's best left to other rounds
The patient, well-aware souls
Will last stone for pound!

Up Not Out

[Written 10 Sept 2009]

Quiet Like the lake at 3 A.M.
Unwavering, your goal to make
Every, second—just squirm on by
Each tear shed, alone in our
Nap sack; our cold, lonely bed.
Awaken those feelings of
Careful love, caress in hug
Time wit you, I will shrug
Intelligent guess, you're from above
Now, I pray your day goes smooth
Good tidings sent your way

Peace, food-& drink aplenty!
Respect from your peers, family!
In everything, give thanks and
Nod or shake, uncertainty quakes!
Caught a glimpse of your aura
Energy beyond quota, a star
Sears your image to my psyche
So good, like in the movies, Mikey.

Spiky hair or flowin', I don't
Care, long as you're goin'
All ways are good when blessed
Reality is toughest test
End your pity party, now! The
Dire shadows of old brows
Old traditions, old may get stale
Flick off dust; of tired trail

Beckoning you into the light
Eyes sparkle both day and night
Increasing stature with good deeds
Nimblest of creature feeds
Got to tell the world, I'm good!

Scenes abound & people could-
Care a bit about the buffer
Around your fence, behind your fluffer
Regulate amounts of fun & sun-
Rays give that-D-vitaMON (Yeah, Mon)
Erase the cold & bitter past
Develop YOU, you're free at last.

Wolf Den

[Quoted from and Written November 1-2, 2007]

He raped me of my pride
And I'm supposed to let that slide?!
I think you're all in for a wild ride,
If you think I'll toss this aside
All these feelings that I hide
And this isht all coincides
With what the heCK is going on
Inside my head. You don't know, I do. Stay out!
I would not dare go down that route.
You will not see me falter
You will not hear me fall
I'm listening for my call
And if I stop, you'll have a ball
As my pack watches me stall.
Fear me, if you will
Laugh at me, if you may
I really don't care,
But you are part of my decay
So as I idly sit and wait and listen
I know you're wishin'

That I'd be missin'
But you're wishing the wrong wish
'Cause I'm here to balance this dish
A rare breed must avoid certain death
Snakes in grass rue the day they cross my path
I am not extinct, yet
And you will NOT bring upon my extinction
With your vicious, malicious attacks
Behind my back
AT MY BACK
That will not loosen the slack
Or diminish your attack
My angels watch my back
Believe me, their deck is stacked
Omnipresent in all I do
In case you forgot, I am not yet through.

"Hell hath no fury like a woman scorned."-Tupac Amaru Shakur

You Knew

[Written 29 Oct 2007]

There comes a time, in each of our
Ominous paths of life, where we must
Re-evaluate situations and society's
Enthusiastic role in our development.

Interrogate the system, unless you
Need blind faith to guide. Remember,

That it is consistently blind and the
Weak leading the weaker ends in
Otherwise tragic results. Even the

Tired, blurred, can see that when it's
History repeating, then, you are the
Real fool. First time is learning
Or exploring, while second IS copying
Unknowing first. I thirst for more
General details to living proper and
Happiness is my permanent companion.

Love may be our only escape
Inside the monotony of same
Victims change the way they think
In case, unclear, who takes the blame
Neglect loose ties and not wonder the unraveling,
Guess which rope breaks to ease the insanity.

Bar Hopped

[Written 20 Mar 2011, in Dublin, Ireland]

Situations all can be learning
Exist where you stand, land
Always sweet, follow or pound the beat
Now is the time, to live-complete

Only good & Sexy hang with me
Care, love & tenderly livin'
Oh, sighs of relief; heard, sung free
Never a dull second, milli—SEE

November opens floodgates TRUE
Eternal BLiss, and there's girls I miss
Laughter, my medicals, chart they top
Love for life, my heart won't stop

Reflect, fond of memories, pure
Unwrap gift of today, beauty flows
Inside my mind, clarity-fair ride
All currency accepted, on hope slide.

Reality is what YoU make it. Warm it up
Imbibe the higher state-All may find
Fellowship, cart around NICE, vibes MOVE
Resist that nothingness—Ecstasy, found in my kiss
It will soothe, choose better way-LOVE
Everything that smoothly beats life's pulse

No one has felt the passion, here-Warrior
Determined to thrive, in the hollow of God's hand.

City of Angels native, Cris "BL!ss", has been writing, creatively, since the single digit years. Survivor, Warrior-In-the-Name-of-Love, Peace Ambadassador and Stand-In Single Mother, she has been busy, getting her Passport stamped. Prose and poetry are an extension of her emotions. Thought processes go from Psalms to Ecclesiastes.

Learning survival skills from all walks of life AND teaching others are main objectives, in this nurturing, vibrant soul. Children and animals are drawn to her. When she walks into a room, the entire building lights up.

Bold. Beautiful. Daring. Courageous. Charismatic. Enigmatic. Sporadic. Peace. Love. Faith. Believe. Respect. Freedom. Joy. Bliss.